Utah
on my mind

CAROL POLICH

" *In Utah, we still have islands of visible, palpable uniqueness. Here you can taste and feel color; the sheer immensity of distance becomes intimate. This land is remote, prickly, painfully beautiful.* "

Ellen Meloy

The Globe Pequot Press

Guilford, Connecticut

A soothing swath of lupine grows below Devil's Castle Peak in the Wasatch Range.   STEPHEN TRIMBLE

" *The solitude, the stillness, the subdued light, and the vastness of every surrounding object, produce an impression of awe....* "

Joseph Christmas Ives, 1858

The warbling song of the mountain bluebird is a birder's delight. GARY CRANDALL

Flaming bigtooth maples frame the Stewart Cascades in 10,750-acre Mount Timpanogos Wilderness. TOM TILL

Remnants of an autumn rain reflect the monolith known as the Organ, in Arches National Park.   LARRY ULRICH

Sandstone hoodoos provide a backdrop for evening primrose and locoweed on the San Rafael Swell near Moab.   JACK DYKINGA

66 *All desert plants are emphatic; it is as if by sight or smell they must impress the visitor instantly, since they have their own way to make in the world and cannot depend on man to nurture and preserve them.* 99

Maurine Whipple

Locoweed and yellow cryptantha thrive in the desert, far from the snowfields of the Henry Mountains.   LARRY ULRICH

Clover and compact nama flourish despite their parched
surroundings in the Fremont River Valley.   JACK DYKINGA

Clouds roll over a field littered with coarse volcanic boulders and tough pinyon pines.   SCOTT T. SMITH

A pioneer's dream refuses to die amid wild roses growing in Box Elder County.   SCOTT T. SMITH

Cottonwoods flaunt their autumn finery below the stark slopes of South Cainville Mesa along the Fremont River.   SCOTT T. SMITH

The Green River meanders through rock strata millions of years in the making at Split Mountain Gorge, Dinosaur National Monument.   SCOTT T. SMITH

66 The further our curiosity probes back into the story of the rocks, openly revealed but in a language strange to most of us, the further our imagination is stretched by new revelations, and by a new concept of time. 99

Wallace Stegner

A paleontologist mines the eons at Dinosaur National Monument.   STEWART M. GREEN

You can almost feel the earth shake as you study these well-preserved dinosaur tracks near the Hurricane Cliffs. TOM TILL

Mount Naomi Wilderness encompasses more than 44,000 acres between Logan and Bear Lake. SCOTT T. SMITH

If [the mule deer] sees that he is discovered he can make a dash up or down the mountain in a way that astonishes . . . . His feet seem to strike rubber instead of stone; for he bounds like a ball, describes a quarter circle, and bounds again.

John C. Van Dyke

This mule deer buck must bulk up to survive the winter.
NEIL WEIDNER

In the Bear River Range, the craggy face of Mount Magog peers back at itself from White Pine Lake.   SCOTT T. SMITH

Historically hunters and gatherers, the Navajo today raise sheep and grow crops on their reservation, which sprawls into southeastern Utah.   STEPHEN TRIMBLE

The weatherworn face of a Navajo man reflects the rich history and ruddy desert landscape of his home in Monument Valley.   STEPHEN TRIMBLE

Composed of striking DeChelly sandstone, West Mitten Butte in Monument Valley Tribal Park is sacred to the Navajo people.   LONDIE G. PADELSKY

Gleeful Navajo children board the bus for Head Start.
STEPHEN TRIMBLE

❝ If one is inclined to wonder at first how so many dwellers came to be in the loneliest land that ever came out of God's hands, what they do there and why stay, one does not wonder so much after having lived there. ❞

Mary Austin

In Glen Canyon National Recreation Area, a delicate sandstone caprock formation is burnished by the day's first light.   JACK DYKINGA

Rock climbers flock to Utah to challenge themselves on lofty sandstone towers like Lizard Rock, shown here.   STEWART M. GREEN

Mexican Hat Rock perches precariously above the San Juan River on the Navajo Indian Reservation.   LARRY ULRICH

Gorgeous summer days are made for exploring places like aptly named Lily Lake in the Uinta Mountains.   LONDIE G. PADELSKY

" *Away to the south the Uinta Mountains stretch in a long line,—high peaks thrust into the sky, and snow fields glittering like lakes of molten silver, and pine forests in somber green, and rosy clouds playing around the borders of huge, black masses; and heights and clouds and mountains and snow fields and forests and rocklands are blended into one grand view.* "

John Wesley Powell, 1869

The warmth of the sun lures a painted turtle topside.
JOHN R. FORD

A belly float allows this angler to quietly explore the nooks and crannies of
Blind Lake in the Dixie National Forest.   SCOTT T. SMITH

The Green River in northeastern Utah is a favorite among trout fishermen.   FRANK JENSEN

A handsome brook trout culled from North Eden Creek will make a delicious dinner for some lucky angler.   JAMES KIRK GARDNER

" One great thing about fly-fishing is that after a while nothing exists in the world but thoughts about fly-fishing. "

Norman Maclean

Utah is renowned for its autumn displays of aspen trees, resplendent here among the Engelmann spruce on the banks of Flatiron Lake. SCOTT T. SMITH

> *Something like a yellow rash has broken out upon the mountainsides—the aspen forests in their autumn splendor.*

Edward Abbey

A nuthatch gets a new outlook on life while suspended beak-down from a pinecone. JOHN R. FORD

23

The bold white trunks of aspen trees provide a pleasing contrast to masses of fall foliage in the Wasatch Range.   BRUCE TREMPER

Mount Timpanogos is one of the most popular peaks for climbing in Utah.   LARRY ULRICH

Taking young children hiking can instill a love of the outdoors that will last their entire lives.   HOWIE GARBER

Though its life revolves around water, the wood duck prefers to nest in the trees.   JOHN R. FORD

Fish Creek cuts a channel through the red sandstone of Cedar Mesa, LEON WERDINGER

Founded by Mormons in 1859, Logan is the seat of Cache County and the home of Utah State University.   SCOTT T. SMITH

Named in honor of LDS leader Brigham Young, Brigham City nestles
at the foot of the Wellsville Mountains.   SCOTT T. SMITH

Park City is perhaps best known as the site of the Sundance Film Festival, which annually turns Main Street into a concourse for the rich and famous.   STEPHEN TRIMBLE

Nucor Steel in Plymouth manufactures rolled steel, joists, girders, decks, grinding balls, and other steel components. SCOTT T. SMITH

Every day is the Fourth of July for a steel cutter in the Nucor mill.　SCOTT T. SMITH

Thiokol Propulsion in Ogden makes the solid rocket motors used to boost the space shuttle from its launch pad.   SCOTT T. SMITH

Billed as the world's largest open-pit mine, the Bingham Copper Mine in the Oquirrh Mountains near Salt Lake City has produced billions of dollars worth of ore.   SCOTT T. SMITH

As the sun rose slowly above the eastern horizon, the caps of the great mountains lit up one after the other, like lamps at a festival, until they were all ruddy and glowing.

Sir Arthur Conan Doyle

The Rocky Mountain elk thrives throughout the state and is the official state animal.   JOHN R. FORD

Sun and clouds kiss the summit of Superior Peak in the Twin Peaks Wilderness. TOM TILL

Pillows of snow surround these cottonwood trees at the Snowbasin Ski Area near Ogden. KATHLEEN NORRIS COOK

The shy and stealthy cougar moves as silently as snow through the Utah backcountry. GARY CRANDALL

Winter dresses a stand of ponderosa pines in pompoms of frost.   JACK DYKINGA

Winter has settled down over the Divide again; the season in which Nature recuperates, in which she sinks to sleep between the fruitfulness of autumn and the passion of spring.

Willa Cather

> *The few cliff-dwellings he had seen—all ruins—had left him with haunting memory of age and solitude and of something past. He had come, in a way, to be a cliff-dweller himself, and those silent eyes would look down upon him, as if in surprise that after thousands of years a man had invaded the valley.*

Zane Grey

Hikers in Zion National Park make sure they can always find a spot of shade.   SCOTT T. SMITH

The remnant of an ancient Pueblo civilization clings to the cliffs above the Virgin River in Zion National Park.   TOM TILL

A hiker is suitably impressed by the immensity of Double Arch Alcove in Zion National Park. JACK OLSON

66 *At first look it all seems like a geologic chaos, but there is method at work here, method of a fanatic order and perseverance; each groove in the rock leads to a natural channel of some kind, every channel to a ditch and gulch and ravine, each larger waterway to a canyon bottom or broad wash leading in turn to the Colorado River and the sea.* 99

Edward Abbey

Indian paintbrushes make their move on Checkerboard Mesa, a petrified sand dune. MICHAEL SAMPLE

The Virgin River carves a solitary course through Zion National Park on its way to Lake Mead.   TONY LITSCHEWSKI

The Subway was named for its erosion pattern, which looks like a subway tunnel, and from the roar of the water, which sounds like a subway train.   AARON GOLDENBERG

Bizarre rock formations, like these in Squaw Canyon, define the landscape of Canyonlands National Park.   LARRY ULRICH

With its sharp, spiny leaves and graceful blooms, the yucca is a desert paradox.   LONDIE G. PADELSKY

Morning light seeps into the serpentine canyon of the Colorado River in Dead Horse Point State Park.   TOM TILL

" The Canyon curves deeply to the left and right, sinuous as a snake, no more willing to follow a straight line than anything else true and beautiful and good in this world. "

Edward Abbey

Gambel oaks and bigtooth maples litter the floor of Clear Creek Canyon. LARRY ULRICH

" To-day we are among forests of rare beauty and luxuriance; the air is moist and cool, the grasses are green and rank, and hosts of flowers deck the turf like the hues of a Persian carpet. "

Clarence E. Dutton, 1869

A mule deer and a bigtooth maple both leave their calling cards on a sandy stream bed. JEFF FOOTT

A mist settles over Upper Emerald Pool Falls in Zion National Park.   LARRY ULRICH

The State Capitol, completed in 1915, serves as a beacon to Salt Lake motorists scurrying home at dusk.   SCOTT T. SMITH

" Salt Lake is an easy town to know. . . . Lying in a great bowl valley, it can be surmounted and comprehended and possessed wholly as few cities can. You can't possibly get lost in it. The Wasatch comes with such noble certitude up from the south and curves so snugly around the 'Avenues' that from anywhere in the city you can get your directions and find your way. "

Wallace Stegner

Utah's governor resides at the Kearns Mansion, built by an early mining baron who founded the *Salt Lake Tribune*.   STEPHEN TRIMBLE

City Creek Park provides a quiet respite from the hustle and bustle of downtown Salt Lake City.   SCOTT T. SMITH

The world-famous Mormon Tabernacle Choir is made up of 320 volunteers,
each of whom is limited to 20 years of service.   STEPHEN TRIMBLE

*" Salt Lake City is a divided concept, a complex idea. To the
devout it is more than a place; it is a way of life, a corner of the
materially realizable heaven; its soil is held together by the roots
of the family and the cornerstones of the temple.* "

Wallace Stegner

Gaily lighted for the Christmas season, the Mormon Temple is the focal point of Salt Lake's Temple Square, as well as the hub of the Church of Latter-day Saints.   SCOTT T. SMITH

The Wasatch Mountains serve as a backdrop for the Gothic turrets of Salt Lake's City-County Building, built in the 1890s and renovated in the 1980s.   SCOTT T. SMITH

Dedicated in 1909, the Cathedral of the Madeleine is the heart of Salt Lake's Catholic community.   SCOTT T. SMITH

Close to 2,000 students attend Westminster College, a private, nondenominational, liberal-arts school founded in Salt Lake City in 1875. SCOTT T. SMITH

The administrative offices of the University of Utah are housed in the distinguished John Park Building, built in 1914. SCOTT T. SMITH

The Great Salt Lake, about eight times saltier than the Pacific Ocean, attracts thousands of waterfowl, including these pelicans.   GARY CRANDALL

Mallards feed like pigs at a trough on the aquatic offerings of the Great Salt Lake.   GARY CRANDALL

Antelope Island, the largest of 10 islands in the Great Salt Lake, is the home of a protected herd of about 600 bison.   TOM TILL

" Ascending to the summit, immediately at our feet [we] beheld the object of our anxious search—the waters of the Inland Sea, stretching in still and solitary grandeur far beyond the limit of our vision.... It was one of the great points of the exploration. "

John Charles Frémont, 1843

For a spectacular bird's-eye view, you can take a gondola ride over Bridal Veil Falls in the Wasatch Range.   JACK OLSON

Bridal Veil Falls in Provo Canyon drops 607 feet in two cascades.   AARON GOLDENBERG

The most famous attraction in Arches National Park is 65-foot-tall Delicate Arch,
once colorfully dubbed "The Schoolmarm's Bloomers."   AARON GOLDENBERG

> " *A weird, lovely, fantastic object out of nature like Delicate Arch has the curious ability to remind us—like rock and sunlight and wind and wilderness—that* out there *is a different world, older and greater and deeper by far than ours, a world which surrounds and sustains the little world of men as sea and sky surround and sustain a ship.* "
>
> Edward Abbey

Photographers vie for the perfect shot of Delicate Arch. BRIAN MILLER

Jeep Arch in Upper Goldbar Canyon frames the snow-dusted peaks of the La Sal Mountains. TONY LITSCHEWSKI

The Hale-Bopp Comet sweeps across the sky above Turret Arch in Arches National Park. TOM TILL

Mule-ears make a flamboyant appearance at Courthouse Towers in Arches National Park. TOM TILL

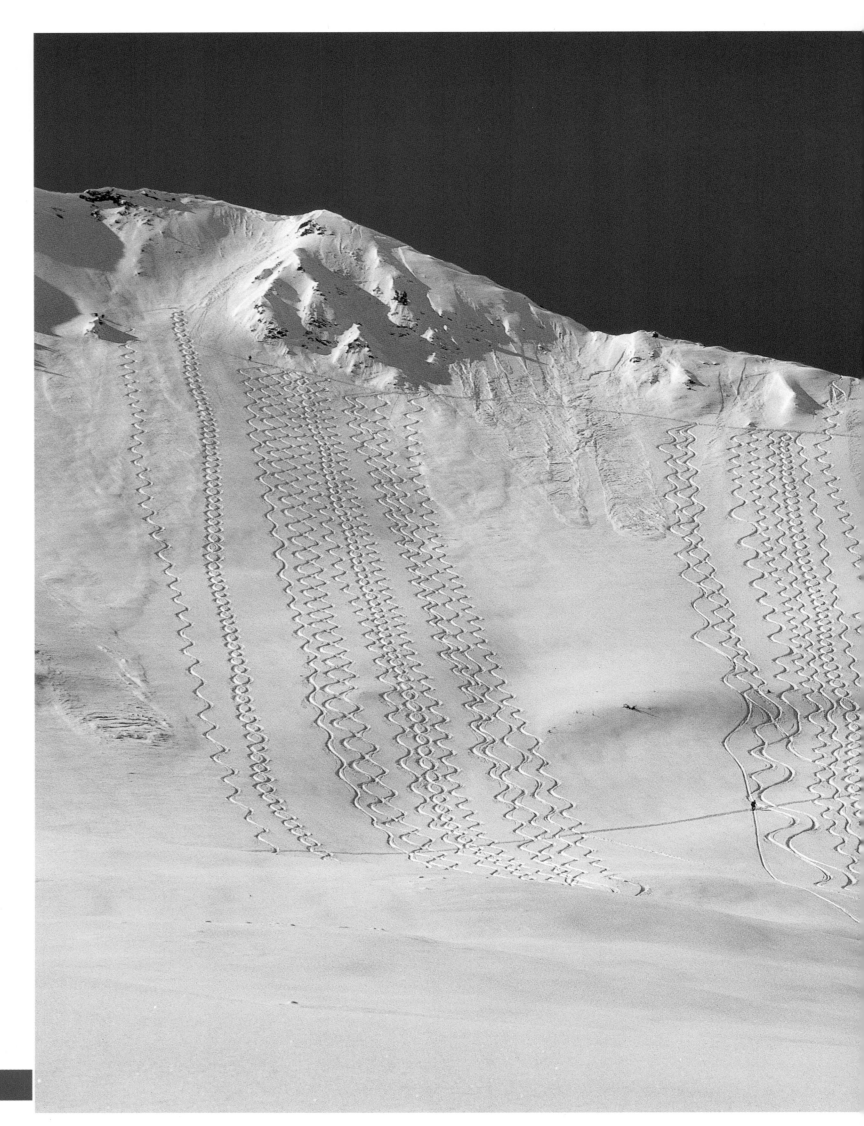

Skiers doodle in the "Greatest Snow on Earth"——the cold, dry powder for which Utah ski areas are famous.   HOWIE GARBER

66 *Skiing down 'between heaven and earth,' each of us was surrounded by a cloud of luminous powder snow, every crystal illuminated by the slanting rays of the setting sun. Total bliss all the way!* 99

Dolores LaChapelle

Fourteen Utah ski areas, most on the Wasatch Front, attract skiers young and old. STEPHEN TRIMBLE

A skier tests an Olympic freestyle course in Deer Valley, once described as "the crème de la crème of ski destinations." STEPHEN TRIMBLE

" Tired, nerve shaken, over-civilized people are beginning to find out that going to the mountains is going home; that wilderness is a necessity; and that mountain parks and reservations are useful not only as fountains of timber and irrigating rivers, but as fountains of life. "

John Muir

Park City, Utah's largest ski resort, will host several events during the 2002 Winter Olympic Games. CHEYENNE ROUSE

A backcountry skier delights in fresh snow and astounding views on Kessler Ridge in the Wasatch Mountains. HOWIE GARBER

Utah ski areas—and skiers—welcome an average of 300 to 500 inches of snow a year. HOWIE GARBER

Ice crystals create bizarre but beautiful patterns in Arches National Park.   GARY CRANDALL

*⁶⁶ My travels have taken me
often, and always by car, across the
fabulous landscape of Utah. It is
awesomely beautiful. I say to myself
as I gaze about me, 'It must take
courage to live in such beauty.' ⁹⁹*

Pearl Buck

Ice climbers scale frozen cascades in Provo Canyon
south of Salt Lake City.   HOWIE GARBER

Frigid fingers "play" the Organ, one of many unique rock formations in Arches National Park.   JACK DYKINGA

A cowboy trails some dust-kickin' dogies in Capitol Reef National Park.   STEPHEN TRIMBLE

> " *There is an easy comfort given to believers of the Western dream, knowing that cowboys are, at this very moment, galloping around somewhere, roping sick stock, and sleeping out under the stars.* "
>
> Kurt Markus

A cowboy reflects on the solitary life on the Utah range.
WILSON GOODRICH

In Bicknell, the smiles of children brighten a float in the annual Pioneer Day parade.   STEPHEN TRIMBLE

A young Indian dancer dons traditional dress for a veteran's
parade in Salt Lake City.   STEPHEN TRIMBLE

Modern "pioneers" in traditional garb celebrate the centennial of Utah's statehood in 1996.   SCOTT T. SMITH

"Aw shucks," this young cowpoke seems about to say.
WILSON GOODRICH

The Heber Creeper locomotive hauls sightseers back in time as it steams through Heber Valley and Provo Canyon.   FRANK JENSEN

Engineers demonstrate the inner workings of the Heber Creeper as it chugs toward Bridal Veil Falls.   FRANK JENSEN

At Golden Spike National Historic Site, train replicas re-enact the momentous completion in 1869 of the first transcontinental railroad. JACK OLSON

" *The last rail is laid. The last spike is driven. The Pacific railroad is finished.* "

1869 telegraph message
sent from Promontory Summit

A backpacker follows sinuous sandstone ribbons through southern Utah's canyon country.   JOHN DITTLI

Utah's unique and diverse landscape has prompted some to call it the "mountain biking capital of the nation." HOWIE GARBER

Shooting the rapids of Desolation Canyon, on the Green River,
is sure to give rafters a thrill. TED WOOD

Utah Highway 95 twists and turns along the meandering shore of Lake Powell, the second largest manmade reservoir in the world.   JACK DYKINGA

Most of Lake Powell's 1,960-mile shoreline is accessible only by boat.   TED WOOD

Nature throws a spotlight on the waters of Lake Powell. KATHLEEN NORRIS COOK

Day's end finds this Green River paddler glowing with the dying light and the thrill of adventure.   SCOTT T. SMITH

Who knows what monstrous creatures lurk in the muddy San Juan River?   LEON WERDINGER

Before turning in, a gutsy backpacker enjoys the advantages of his room with a view.   CHEYENNE ROUSE

This family hasn't got cold feet about exploring the Escalante River.   STEPHEN TRIMBLE

>**"** *I have not tired of the wilderness; rather I enjoy its beauty and the vagrant life I lead, more keenly all the time. I prefer… star-sprinkled sky to a roof, the obscure and difficult trail, leading into the unknown, to any paved highway, and the deep peace of the wild to the discontent bred by cities. Do you blame me then for staying here, where I feel that I belong and am one with the world around me?* **"**
>
> Everett Ruess

A new day bursts into Canyonlands National Park by way of Mesa Arch.   SCOTT T. SMITH

The Three Gossips exchange secrets in Arches National Park.   MICHAEL SAMPLE

66 *It is the kingdom of sun-fire. For every color in the scale is attuned to the key of flame, every airwave comes with the breath of flame, every sunbeam falls as a shaft of flame. There is no questioning who is sovereign in these dominions.* **99**

John C. Van Dyke

Look but don't touch the fiery blossoms of the prickly pear cactus.   HOWIE GARBER

Fog storms the ramparts at Castle Peak in the proposed La Sal Waters Wilderness.   TOM TILL

> *When speaking of these rocks, we must not conceive of piles of boulders, or heaps of fragments, but a whole land of naked rock, with giant forms carved on it: cathedral-shaped buttes, towering hundreds or thousands of feet; cliffs that cannot be scaled, and cañon walls... with vast, hollow domes, and tall pinnacles... all highly colored buff, gray, red, brown, and chocolate....*

John Wesley Powell

The long ears of the jackrabbit radiate body heat and help to keep it cool.   WILSON GOODRICH

Water seeping through Death Hollow in the Escalante area allows red algae to flourish.   JACK DYKINGA

66 *The little canyon resembles a Japanese garden embroidered with a narrow thread of water. The walls are shiny black schist, veined with white lines or brown bands, brush strokes of orange, thumbprints of white, wispy traces of gray. Boulders judiciously rounded and exquisitely placed cause the water to whisper and gossip.... Sound transforms to moving light, concentric circles echo off a wall like musical chimes, a gentle little stream playing with its reflections.* 99

Ann Haymond Zwinger

The lifeblood of the Utah desert, water cascades over Lower Calf Creek Falls in
Grand Staircase-Escalante National Monument. JEFF FOOTT

Mount Ogden presides over a pastoral scene near Huntsville.   STEPHEN TRIMBLE

A farmer oils a working steam thresher on the Ronald Jensen
Historic Farm in Cache Valley.   SCOTT T. SMITH

An old barn rests at the base of the Wellsville Mountains near Mendon.   SCOTT T. SMITH

A western screech owl peeks from its penthouse on the roof of a barn.   HOWIE GARBER

A mountain goat scrambles easily down a scree slope in the Mount Timpanogos
Wilderness Area northwest of Orem.   HOWIE GARBER

When your spirit cries for peace, come to a world of canyons deep in an old land; feel the exultation of the high plateaus, the strength of moving waters, the simplicity of sand and grass, and the silence of growth.

August Frugé

A marmot serves sentry duty in the Uinta Mountains.
MICHAEL SAMPLE

85

Fir trees skirt Red Mountain in the Deep Creek Range near the Utah-Nevada border. STEPHEN TRIMBLE

Two bull moose share a quiet moment among the willows. GARY CRANDALL

Wheeler Creek hurdles headlong among the aspens in Snow Basin, the Wasatch Range. STEPHEN TRIMBLE

Lightning dances over the Wellsville Mountains in northcentral Utah.   SCOTT T. SMITH

Turbulent clouds threaten a downpour in Cache Valley, northcentral Utah.   SCOTT T. SMITH

An afternoon rainstorm creates ephemeral falls and softens the silhouette of Kolob Canyon. FRANK JENSEN

“ The bank of clouds now swept hugely out of the western sky. Its front was purple and black, with gray between, a bulging, mushrooming, vast thing instinct with storm.... As if all the power of the winds were pushing and piling behind, it rolled ponderously across the sky. ”

Zane Grey

Nature dips a finger into Margo Lake, at the base of Mount Agassiz in the High Uintas Wilderness Area.   SCOTT T. SMITH

The Uintas, among the wildest and most rugged mountains in the West, gently cradle Moosehorn Lake.   NEIL WEIDNER

Utahns are known to be industrious, and this busy beaver is no exception.   JOHN R. FORD

A ponderosa pine pierces a slot canyon along the Navajo Loop Trail in Bryce Canyon National Park.   JACK OLSON

The morning sun plays peek-a-boo among the siltstone spires of Bryce Canyon National Park. JACK DYKINGA

Riders explore the hoodoos and canyons of Bryce Canyon National Park, described by some as the most colorful park in the world. CAROL POLICH

While generations of humans work, eat, sleep, and play, Coyote Creek continues to sculpt soft sandstone in Glen Canyon National Recreation Area.   JACK DYKINGA

" Here, sun, wind, and rain have played with the brilliant, multicolored land for a billion years, leaving the recorded history of the earth's beginnings on a complex landscape of plateaus, cliffs, buttes, and river-cut canyon walls. "

Karen Shephard

Circular spillways serve as natural skylights in Neon Canyon, Glen Canyon National Recreation Area.   JACK DYKINGA

A desert tortoise is unimpressed by the menacing spines of a prickly pear.   JAMES KIRK GARDNER

" Anything that lives where it would seem that nothing could live, enduring extremes of heat and cold, sunlight and storm, parching aridity and sudden cloudbursts, among burnt rock and shifting sands, any such creature—beast, bird or flower—testifies to the grandeur and heroism inherent in all forms of life. "

Edward Abbey

The collared lizard owes its name to its characteristic bright throat patch.   JOHN DITTLI

Horseback riding through the foothills of the La Sal Mountains is a popular form
of recreation for locals and tourists alike.   FRANK JENSEN

A three-room Anasazi ruin on Cedar Mesa is a haunting reminder of those who came before. LONDIE G. PADELSKY

Petroglyphs in Arches National Park stir the imagination and leave us to wonder what life was like 1,000 years ago. LONDIE G. PADELSKY

The ghost of an Anasazi appears to sweep into a ruin on Cedar Mesa.
JOHN DITTLI

66 *Silence. That is time you are hearing. We are in Anasazi country. This is a place where canyon walls rise upward like praying hands. Veins of water run between them.... This is the landscape that gave these people birth.* 99

Terry Tempest Williams

Hairpin turns compete with magnificent sandstone ramparts for a driver's attention in Canyonlands. CAROL POLICH

No one knows what became of the ancient peoples who fashioned the pottery from which these fragments came. JOHN DITTLI

A ruin with a view—who wouldn't want to call this land home? TOM TILL

All that remains of the town of Thistle are a few dilapidated buildings—and the thistles.   TOM TILL

66 Artifacts are alive. Each has a voice. They remind us what it means to be human—that it is our nature to survive, to create works of beauty, to be resourceful, to be attentive to the world we live in. **99**

Terry Tempest Williams

The Festival of the American West, held annually in Logan, celebrates the lifestyles of the pioneers.   FRANK JENSEN

Ghost towns are scattered throughout Utah; this one rests in peace near the Paria River in the recently designated Grand Staircase-Escalante National Monument.   TOM TILL

These pieces of the past, found in an abandoned cabin in Desolation Canyon, affirm the suitability of the area's name.   BRUCE TREMPER

Salt not snow encrusts a tumbleweed on the.north shore of the Great Salt Lake.   SCOTT T. SMITH

The new ice age? No, it's the Bonneville Salt Flats in northern Utah, devoid of most life but home to shimmering mirages.   FRANK JENSEN

Each year, racers from around the world attempt to set new land-speed records at the Bonneville Salt Flats.   FRANK JENSEN

" *How [the salt flat] glares like snowfields under the sun, how it glimmers and quivers in the snaky heat waves and fills the plain with lakes that quench no thirst.* "

Bernard De Voto

The Castle rises above the visitor center in Capitol Reef National Park, which was established in 1937 and is Utah's least-visited national park.　JEFF FOOTT

The rising sun pays homage at the Temple of the Sun and Moon in Capitol Reef National Park.　JEFF FOOTT

More than 100 years ago, pioneers engraved their names on this rock—an act that today would earn a hefty fine or even a jail term. JEFF FOOTT

66 The landscape that is the simplest in form and the finest in color is by all odds the most beautiful. 99

John C. Van Dyke

Snowmelt from the Uinta Mountains drains north into Wyoming and then returns
to Utah via the Green River and Flaming Gorge.   SCOTT T. SMITH

John Wesley Powell

A fish dinner is on the menu for this bald eagle.
GARY CRANDALL

Cheery primrose blossoms brighten Bryce Canyon National Park. FRANK JENSEN

" The desert floras shame us with their cheerful adaptations to the seasonal limitations. Their whole duty is to flower and fruit, and they do it hardly, or with tropical luxuriance, as the rain admits. "

Mary Austin

Springtime brings out the best in these prickly-pear cactuses.
HOWIE GARBER

The moon peeks through a gap in the rock formations of Arches National Park.   KATHLEEN NORRIS COOK

A primrose greets the new day in Capitol Reef National Park.   WILSON GOODRICH

The mirrorlike surface of the Bear River doubles the pleasure of a serene spring day in the Cache Valley.   SCOTT T. SMITH

He may be cute, but he is definitely not cuddly.   JOHN R. FORD

A lone tumbleweed stops short among the monkeyflowers on the shore of Bear Lake.   SCOTT T. SMITH

Lake Blanche whiles away the centuries at the foot of Sundial Peak in Big Cottonwood Canyon.   AARON GOLDENBERG

The rocky cliffs of southeastern Utah provide perfect habitat for the sure-footed bighorn.   MICHAEL SAMPLE

The deer mouse is probably the most common mammal in Utah.
JOHN R. FORD

❝ Once in a while an inert, grayish brown piece of rock will turn and reveal a curve of white rump, white bands down slender legs as smooth as smoke, and there it is, a bighorn, a Fremont or Anasazi petroglyph come alive. ❞

Ellen Meloy

they made it possible

Utah on My Mind would have been impossible to produce without the keen eyes and technical skills of more than two dozen professional photographers. These women and men submitted their finest images, and the results show in this stunning collection of photos. What does not show is the work it took to get these images—the early mornings to capture the sunrise, the long hikes through deep snow and desert, the endless hours of waiting for the perfect light, the hundreds of shots that didn't turn out quite right, and the high level of technical skill that was acquired through years of experience and study. To all the photographers who contributed to *Utah on My Mind,* we say thanks. We appreciate their art and their hard work.

The Globe Pequot Press

Photographers in *Utah on My Mind*

Kathleen Norris Cook
John Dittli
Jack Dykinga
Jeff Foott
John R. Ford
Howie Garber
James Kirk Gardner
Wilson Goodrich
Stewart M. Green
David Jensen
Frank Jensen
Tony Litschewski
Brian Miller
Jack Olson
Londie G. Padelsky
Carol Polich
Cheyenne Rouse
Michael Sample
Scott T. Smith
Tom Till
Bruce Tremper
Stephen Trimble
Larry Ulrich
Neil Weidner
Leon Werdinger
Ted Wood

Dancing Crane Productions
  Gary Crandall
  Aaron Goldenberg

ISBN 1-56044-694-3

Manufactured in Korea
First Edition/Fourth Printing

www.globe-pequot.com

Text research: Don McIvor
Front cover photo:
  Capitol Reef National Park CAROL POLICH
Front cover inset photo: California gull JEFF FOOTT
Back cover photos:
  Bryce Canyon National Park TOM TILL
  Downhill skier HOWIE GARBER
  Sundial Peak and Lake Blanche AARON GOLDENBERG
  Utah State Capitol and Morman Temple FRANK JENSEN
End papers: Canyonlands National Park JEFF FOOTT

acknowledgments

Pages 1 and 96 quotes from *Testimony: Writers of the West Speak on Behalf of Utah Wilderness*, compiled by Stephen Trimble and Terry Tempest Williams. Minneapolis: Milkweed Editions, 1996.

Page 3 quote as reprinted in *Raven's Exile*, by Ellen Meloy. New York: Henry Holt and Company, 1994.

Page 6 quote from *The Giant Joshua*, by Maurine Whipple. Boston: Houghton Mifflin, 1942.

Page 10 quote from *This Is Dinosaur: Echo Park Country and Its Magic Rivers,* ed. by Wallace Stegner. Boulder, CO: Roberts Rhinehart, 1985.

Pages 12, 77, and 109 quotes from *The Desert*, by John C. Van Dyke. Salt Lake City: Peregrine Smith, 1980.

Pages 15 and 112 quotes from *The Land of Little Rain*, by Mary Austin. Boston and New York: Houghton Mifflin, 1903.

Pages 19, 79, 93, and 111 quotes from *The Exploration of the Colorado River and Its Canyons*, by John Wesley Powell. New York: Dover Publications, 1961. Originally published in 1875.

Page 21 quote from *A River Runs Through It and Other Stories*, by Norman Maclean. Chicago: University of Chicago Press, 1976.

Pages 23, 38, and 55 quotes from *Desert Solitaire: A Season in the Wilderness*, by Edward Abbey. New York: McGraw-Hill, 1968.

Page 32 quote from "A Study in Scarlet," by Sir Arthur Conan Doyle, in *The Complete Sherlock Holmes*. Garden City, NY: Doubleday and Company, 1960.

Page 35 quote from *O Pioneers!* by Willa Cather. Boston: Houghton Mifflin, 1933.

Pages 36 and 89 quotes from *Riders of the Purple Sage*, by Zane Grey. Roslyn, NY: Walter J. Black, Inc., 1940. Originally published in 1912.

Page 41 quote from *Slickrock*, by Edward Abbey. San Francisco: Sierra Club, 1971.

Page 42 quote from *Report on the Geology of the High Plateaus of Utah*, by Clarence E. Dutton. Washington, DC: Government Printing Office, 1880.

Pages 44 and 46 quotes from *The Sound of Mountain Water*, by Wallace Stegner. New York: Doubleday, 1969.

Pages 51 and 62 quotes as reprinted in *America the Beautiful: Utah*, by Betty McCarthy. Chicago: Childrens Press, 1990.

Page 59 quote from *Deep Powder Snow*, by Dolores LaChapelle. Durango, CO: Kivaki Press, 1993.

Page 60 quote as reprinted in *The Wild West*, by the editors of Time-Life Books. New York: Time-Life Books, 1993.

Page 65 quote from *Buckaroo*, by Kurt Markus. Boston: Little, Brown and Company, 1987.

Page 75 quote from *Everett Ruess: A Vagabond for Beauty*, by W. L. Rusho. Layton, UT: Gibbs Smith Publisher, 1983.

Page 80 quote from *Downcanyon*, by Ann Haymond Zwinger. Tucson: University of Arizona Press, 1995.

Page 85 quote as reprinted in *Rock Climbing: Desert Rock III*, by Eric Bjornstad. Helena, MT: Falcon Publishing, 1999.

Page 98 quote from *Beyond the Wall: Essays from the Outside*, by Edward Abbey. New York: Holt, Rinehart and Winston, 1971.

Page 101 quote from *Pieces of White Shell: A Journey to Navajoland*, by Terry Tempest Williams. New York: Charles Scribner's Sons, 1983.

Page 104 quote from *Refuge*, by Terry Tempest Williams. New York: Pantheon Books, 1991.

Page 107 quote from *The Year of Decision: 1846*, by Bernard De Voto. Boston: Little, Brown and Company, 1943.

Page 117 quote from *Raven's Exile,* by Ellen Meloy. New York: Henry Holt and Company, 1994.

Page 120 quote from *Roughing It*, by Mark Twain. Berkeley: University of California Press, 1996. Originally published in 1872.

Balanced Rock in Arches National Park bids adieu to another glorious day in Utah.   MICHAEL SAMPLE

" *This was fairyland to us, to all intents and purposes—a
land of enchantment, and goblins, and awful mystery.* "

Mark Twain